Effective Domestic Debt Management in Developing Countries

A Compendium prepared by the Economic and Legal Advisory Services Division of the Commonwealth Secretariat

Debt Management Series No.1

Commonwealth Secretariat,
Marlborough House,
Pall Mall, London SW1Y 5HX
United Kingdom

Published by the Commonwealth Secretariat
Designed by *Allen* Lebon
Printed in the United Kingdon by Safair Print Services Ltd.
Wherever possible, the Commonwealth Secretariat uses paper sourced from sustainable forests or from sources that minimise a destructive impact on the environment.

Copies of this publication can be ordered direct from:
Vale Packaging Ltd, 420 Vale Road, Tonbridge, Kent TN9 1TD,
United Kingdom.
Tel: +44 (0)1732 359387
Fax: +44 (0)1732 770620
E-mail: vale@vale-ltd.co.uk

Price: £10.99

ISBN: 0-85092-581-9

Web sites: http//www.thecommonwealth.org
http//www.youngcommonwealth.org
http//www.csdrms.co.uk

Contents

Boxes

Foreword

The management of domestic debt is becoming a major policy issue in many Commonwealth countries. As part of its advisory services in debt and development resource management, the Economic and Legal Advisory Services Division (ELAS) of the Commonwealth Secretariat has held three workshops on Effective Domestic Debt Management: in June 1996 for the Caribbean region, in December 1996 for countries from the Asia–Pacific region, and in March 1998 for African countries. Their object was to help developing Commonwealth countries to manage their domestic debt more effectively by discussing the issues involved and learning from each others' experience.

This report is a compendium of the discussions and papers read at these workshops. The first two parts review the issues involved in domestic debt management for countries whose financial markets are not fully developed. The third part is a checklist of measures that the delegates agreed should be taken to improve domestic debt management in their countries. While acknowledging that a sound analytical framework must be the basis for any thorough discussion of domestic debt management, we have generally tried to avoid a too theoretical approach. The emphasis is on practical issues.

This compendium is prepared to influence both thought and action at a time when the future conduct of domestic debt management operations in many developing countries is in a state of change. We hope that the policy makers in the central banks, and ministries of finance will find this compendium useful. We would welcome any comments on this publication.

M. A. Malik
Director
Economic and Legal Advisory Services Division
Commonwealth Secretariat

Acknowledgements

The compendium was put together by Shekhar Das under the guidance of a staff team of the Economic and Legal Advisory Services Division of the Commonwealth Secretariat, comprising Raj Kumar, Ranee Jayamaha, Dev Useree and Andrew Kitili. Besides ELAS staff, inputs for the background papers commissioned by Economic and Legal Advisory Services Division were from H. K. Pradhan and Colin Kirkpatrick, resource persons from other institutions, as well as from country papers.

This publication has been funded through the operational arm of the Commonwealth Secretariat, the Commonwealth Fund for Technical Co-operation.

1. Effective Domestic Debt Management in Developing Countries

In the 1980s the major problem facing many developing countries was how to deal with external debt. Domestic debt was relatively insignificant and little discussed. This situation has changed. Domestic debt levels have risen, often in the very same countries which faced acute external debt problems. This has implications for both stabilisation and policies aimed at dealing with external debt. How to manage domestic debt, therefore, has become an important issue.

Public domestic debt is the debt a government incurs through borrowing in its own currency from residents of its country. Government bonds or bills represent assets to their holders, but they are simultaneously a liability to the taxpayers who must ultimately redeem them. This basic idea admits of considerable variations:

Domestic debt transfers resources within a country

- The definition could be widened by including the debt not just of central government, but also that of local or provincial governments, state-owned enterprises and agencies whose borrowing is guaranteed by central government. This would be the consolidated debt of the public sector, including the monetary authorities.
- One may wish to exclude the central government's debt to the central bank, which in practice is often not repaid, and is a measure of monetisation.
- One may wish to make a distinction between gross debt and net debt, where we net out of gross debt capital assets of the government and its loans and advances to other sectors.

It does not increase real resources

The key distinction is between internal borrowing by the state authorities and external borrowing. Internal borrowing does not increase the real resources of the country: residents of that country merely give up purchasing power in return for government securities. There is therefore a transfer of purchasing power within the country over the same stock of real resources. External borrowing, on the other hand, allows the import of real resources from abroad. Internal borrowing leads to domestic debt.

However, this clear distinction is somewhat complicated by the fact that foreign investors sometimes invest in the domestic debt instruments of the government. The government's obligations, therefore, are to foreigners, but in its own currency.

Governments use a number of instruments to raise funds. They include the following:

- **Treasury bills**: these are short-term obligations of up to one year.
- **Government notes and bonds**: these are debt instruments over one year or more.
- **Loans**: many governments borrow from banks and residents in their countries.
- **Promissory notes**: these are conditional promises to pay a specific sum on specific dates which some governments in developing countries issue to their creditors and suppliers.
- **Overdrafts or advances from the central bank**: in some countries this can constitute a large proportion of the debt.
- **Savings certificates**: these are non-marketable debt instruments, usually for the retail public.

Government debt is typically held by the central bank, the commercial banks, institutions such as insurance companies and pension and provident funds, and private individuals.

Why domestic debt levels have risen

The external debt crisis is one reason why domestic debt has grown

There are a number of reasons why domestic debt levels have risen to dangerous levels. The external debt crisis has been an important source of the problem for many countries. Governments have had to squeeze domestic demand in order to generate surpluses on the current account of the balance of payments in order to service large external debts. This has led to lower wages and profits, and thus lower tax revenue. Many governments have also encountered deep-seated problems in levying and collecting taxes. Moreover, the moves many have made to liberalise their financial markets have entailed paying higher interest charges on their existing debt, thus exacerbating the pressure on public finances. Finally, many countries have a vast portfolio of loss-making and heavily indebted public sector companies; this puts an additional burden on government debt.

Consequences of excessive borrowing

It is not sound to assume that because domestic debt is owed by the government to its own people and its servicing therefore simply entails a transfer of income from one group to another within the country, it has no undesirable economic consequences. Excessive government borrowing and debt can have a number of bad effects:

The debt burden can slow down the economy

- If the cost of servicing the debt accounts for a large part of government revenue – as it does in many countries – the scope for public spending on desirable items such as health, education and infrastructure is correspondingly diminished.
- If the government pre-empts a large part of the savings of its residents, it may reduce the amount the private sector can borrow or raise in the capital market, thus crowding-out private investment.
- Excessive borrowing can also increase interest rates, thus deterring investment by making it more expensive.
- If the government finances its deficit by borrowing too much from the central bank – through money creation – it stokes up inflation.
- The building up of excessive debt today entails higher servicing costs on future generations who thus suffer higher taxation.
- Excessive domestic debt can affect a country's credit rating and therefore the cost of its future borrowing.
- Finally, domestic debt levels can be built up to levels where they become unsustainable, precipitating an economic crisis.

Objectives of debt management in developing countries

Domestic debt management has different goals in developed and developing countries

It is therefore important for developing countries to learn to manage their domestic debt efficiently. They cannot do so, however, by setting themselves the same objectives as those of debt managers in the advanced countries. Most developing countries are in a radically different situation from advanced countries. In advanced countries, markets for debt securities are highly developed; independent investment institutions have the purchasing capacity and the appetite for government debt; and although there too domestic debt levels have generally risen, macro-economic indicators of fiscal deficits and inflation are not so daunting.

In advanced countries, it is possible to set debt managers a relatively straightforward objective: to cover the government's borrowing needs at the lowest cost. They need not concern themselves with other objectives of government, such as price stability. In practice, in many advanced countries debt management and monetary policy are conducted by the central bank, and the goal, therefore, for debt managers is to minimise the cost of government debt without jeopardising the aims of monetary policy. But in principle at least the two can be separated, and there is a strong argument for thinking that they should be separated institutionally: that the responsibility for debt management should be placed on an independent debt management office and the responsibility for monetary policy should rest on the central bank. In such an arrangement, which exists in Ireland, Sweden and New Zealand, the debt management office aims to minimise the cost of the government's debt, and the central bank aims to keep inflation down to a specified target. They act independently of each other, using different instruments to achieve their ends. Their objectives can be reconciled optimally through the operation of market forces.

A number of objectives have to be reconciled

Such a system is not possible in developing countries, where financial markets are undeveloped, and instruments of both debt management and monetary control are primitive. There will typically be a conflict between borrowing for the government as cheaply as possible and keeping inflation down. Often the right thing to do is to raise interest rates and thus the cost of borrowing.

Moreover, in many developing countries managers cannot simply sell a given quantity of stock of varying maturity and organise the government's portfolio so as to minimise cost and reduce risk. Primary markets for debt securities, if they exist at all, tend to be only for very short-term instruments, such as Treasury bills. Interest rates are typically controlled by the authorities. Secondary markets rarely exist, so there is a lack of the price information that deep and liquid markets provide. The investment institutions such as pension and insurance funds tend to be captives of the authorities: being government-owned, they hold its debt because they are told to. The commercial bank is undercapitalised, bloated with bad loans and typically state-owned.

Close co-ordination with monetary policy is essential

In these circumstances, the operation of debt management is bound to be intimately linked to the operation of monetary policy. Both will initially use the same instruments. Their objectives, therefore, need to be co-ordinated institutionally. That is not all. As remarked above, in many developing countries debt and money have to be managed in an environment where public budgets and inflation are far from stable, and where financial markets are undeveloped. Therefore debt management and monetary policy must also support the common objectives of stabilisation and market development. Specifically, debt managers in developing countries, apart from their primary objective of selling government debt at least cost, should:

- ensure the liquidity needs of the economy are met, as debt management operations have the potential to disrupt the money markets causing short-term interest rate fluctuations;

- support monetary policy by limiting the inflationary impact of deficit financing;
- promote the development of money and capital markets;
- not jeopardise investment by crowding-out the private sector;
- encourage saving by households; and
- act in harmony with external debt management.

Both need to support stabilisation and market development

Conflicts are bound to arise between these objectives. Policy makers need to formulate a clear strategy, taking into account their macro-economic situation and the stage of their market development. And as the situation changes and markets develop, their objectives should change too. Debt management is not a once-and-for-all affair, but an evolving enterprise.

Functions of debt management

Debt management involves a number of inter-related functions:

- **Planning of financing requirements**: projecting government borrowing requirements in the context of fiscal and monetary targets and sustainable levels of debt.
- **Policy**: formulating debt management objectives and strategy; deciding on volume, type of instruments, timing, frequency and selling techniques; where feasible, developing a benchmark debt structure.
- **Primary market organisation (new issues)**: organising distribution channels and selling procedures; managing debt operations including auctions, subscriptions, etc; maintaining close contacts with the market.
- **Secondary market organisation**: actively managing the secondary sales of government's outstanding portfolio; developing these markets; maintaining contacts and intervening in them; encouraging the dealing and dealer systems.
- **Issuance/Redemption**: administration of new and old issues, e.g. delivery and redemption of securities.
- **Administration and accounting**: maintaining an accounting system for debt operations; managing records of debt holders and stock; servicing of government debt; maintaining a register of government debt instruments.
- **Establishing systems**: establishing efficient payments systems, trading procedures and smooth clearing and settlement systems.

Linkages between public debt and fiscal deficits

Several sorts of deficits should be distinguished

The source of public debt lies in budget deficits. If a government spends more than it gets in revenue, it has a deficit. It meets this by borrowing. The cumulative total of its past borrowings is its debt. This is a simple schema, but for practical purposes we need to employ somewhat more complex ideas. To begin with, there are several related concepts of fiscal deficits:

- **Fiscal deficit**: This is the difference between total government spending and total government receipts except those that come from borrowing. On the expenditure side it includes all current non-interest payments, interest payments, capital spending, and net lending. On the income side it includes all tax and non-tax revenues, grants, and receipts from the sale of public sector assets. In other words, it does not distinguish between capital and current income, nor between interest and non-interest expenditure.

  The primary deficit is a key policy target

  The scope of 'government' is unclear in the definition. Is it just the central government, or does it include other parts of the public sector? The World Bank recommends that the borrowing requirement of the whole non-financial public sector should be taken into account, that is, it should include not just the central government, but state or provincial governments, public sector enterprises and the central bank, but exclude financial institutions such as commercial banks which might be owned by the government. This is the measure of deficit adopted by the International Monetary Fund (IMF) as its policy target in its Structural Adjustment Programmes.

- **Revenue or recurrent deficit**: This leaves out from the expenditure side capital items – expenditure which creates assets for the government. The idea is that while current spending and interest payments should be financed from current revenue, capital spending could safely be financed by borrowing.

- **Primary deficit**: This excludes interest payments – the cost of financing past borrowing – from expenditure. This is a key concept in assessing whether a country's debt is sustainable, an issue discussed below.

- **Operational deficit**: This adjusts the fiscal deficit for inflation. Inflation reduces the real value of debt and therefore the interest cost does not reflect the true cost to the government. The operational deficit is the fiscal deficit minus the government's outstanding debt at the beginning of the year multiplied by the inflation rate during the year. This concept is relevant for countries with high rates of inflation where the difference between the fiscal deficit and the operational deficit can be large. (For example, in 1985 Brazil had a fiscal deficit of 27.1 per cent, but an operational deficit of only 3.5 per cent.)

Ways of financing deficits

Fiscal deficits can be financed by borrowing abroad, printing money or borrowing domestically. The sum of these three in any particular year necessarily equals the fiscal deficit for that year. Each of these methods of financing, if carried to excess, can lead to a crisis:

There are three ways of financing a deficit

- **External borrowing** from, for example, foreign governments, multilateral organisations or private institutions, allows a country to import real resources to consume or invest. But the servicing of the debt generated in this way involves transferring resources abroad. Thus the country has to generate an export surplus or borrow further. If the country cannot pay the interest or return the principal when it falls due, it faces a crisis. This is what has happened to several countries during the debt crisis that began in 1982.
- **Borrowing domestically**, within moderate limits, is not inflationary, nor does it have the problems of external borrowing. However, the consequences of excessive domestic borrowing are, as we have mentioned above, undesirable. Moreover, the accumulation of domestic debt as a result of persistent domestic borrowing could reach unsustainable levels. Then the government would have to take painful measures on taxation and spending to bring the debt back to a sustainable level or be plunged into crisis.
- **Borrowing from the central bank** through the sale to it of government securities or other ways such as overdraft advances is a form of money creation: it is just like printing money to pay one's bills.

Carried to excess each leads to problems

There is a degree to which a government can do this without cost and with no bad consequences. In a growing economy the demand for money increases, typically, in proportion to the growth. The government usually has a monopoly over issuing money. It can satisfy this increase in demand by printing money. The profit it makes on this is called seignorage. If, however, it prints more money than the increase in demand for money resulting from growth, it will cause inflation.

To the extent the public accepts this inflation and adapts to rising prices by saving more and increasing its money holdings, the government can get away with this. In effect, the public is willing to be taxed in this way – it is willing to pay an inflation tax. But governments would be foolish to use this form of taxation to excess, for three reasons. First, there is a limit beyond which the yield on this tax falls because the public starts to economise on its money balances. Secondly, high rates of inflation can easily slide into hyper-inflation. Finally, even relatively low rates of inflation disproportionately hurt the poor, an important fact for developing countries.

2. Key Issues for Developing Countries

The experience of developing countries in managing domestic debt shows that there are some pervasive problems which left untackled, or tackled badly, have extremely undesirable consequences.

Domestic debt management – part of overall economic strategy

1. Domestic debt management is often treated in isolation from the rest of macro-economic management. Debt management influences and is influenced by fiscal and monetary policies and the balance of payments. An expansionary fiscal policy, for instance, could raise interest rates and inflation, and thus the cost of public debt. Therefore, at the policy level, debt management should be integrated into an overall strategy which is appropriate for the country.

Revenue reform – part of domestic borrowing strategy

2. Governments face rising fiscal deficits and increasingly rely on domestic borrowing to finance them. Attempts to reduce the deficit run into limitations in the tax base and the demands of spending on development. Tax reform, therefore, has to be implemented at the same time as fiscal adjustment. In the meantime, reliance on bank borrowing boosts money supply and inflation. Attempts to control this produces high real interest rates. Eventually, the public loses confidence in the government's ability to honour its debt obligations.

Need for appropriate borrowing strategy

3. Debt managers often fail to formulate an appropriate borrowing strategy. Borrowing is carried out in a haphazard fashion, without prior deliberation over the alternative methods of funding and a careful consideration of the consequences. As a result, debt managers run into a number of problems which typically include an excessive monetisation of debt, a maturity profile which is very short-term, and a bunching of payments which cause cash flow difficulties.

Need to develop debt securities market

4. Markets for domestic debt instruments are undeveloped. In many countries there is a paucity of debt instruments, the markets for selling them are primitive, mechanisms for trading them inefficient and unreliable, their prices regulated by the government, and the institutions that invest in debt weak. These weaknesses enormously hamper not only debt management, but also monetary management. Debt managers should therefore have an interest in developing markets for debt securities.

Better co-ordination between debt and monetary management

5. There is a lack of co-ordination between debt management and monetary management. There should be close co-ordination between the two because they are intimately linked. One reason lies in the fact that monetary financing of the fiscal deficit is an alternative to debt financing. Another arises from the use by monetary policy of indirect methods of control such as sales and purchases of Treasury bills, which are debt instruments, for its open market operations. Yet in many countries debt managers operate in disharmony with monetary managers.

Better debt monitoring

6. There is a lack of data and a proper mechanism for monitoring debt. This is a serious problem in many countries. Its importance is obvious. Without accurate information available in an appropriate form, effective debt management is not possible.

These problems manifest themselves in a number of ways. Often the stock of debt becomes unsustainable or so large that servicing it entails huge costs to the economy, such as the crowding-out of the private sector, high inflation and a lack of resources for social spending. How to deal with these problems is discussed in detail below.

Six areas for action

1. Integrate debt management into a macro-economic strategy

The debt management policies the government of a country should adopt depend on the situation of the country: on its fiscal and monetary position; its existing stock of debt, both external and domestic; the stage of development of its debt securities markets. What is appropriate for one country will not necessarily be appropriate for another. So the first thing policy makers need to do is to take a good look at their debt in the context of an overall macro-economic framework.

A framework for alternative means of financing fiscal deficit

The framework that is usually adopted is that of the national accounting system where excess savings over investments must finance the excess of public spending (including public investment) over its revenue. Excess spending by the whole economy is possible only when it is financed by the rest of the world. On this basis policy makers can establish an overall projection of fiscal deficits. From this they can derive a borrowing programme, after taking into account estimate of the supply of financial resources in the system, the private sector's demand for credit and the amount of resources available for the public sector that is consistent with the achievement of macro-economic targets. An appropriate assessment of alternative means of financing the deficit must be analysed in detail.

A borrowing strategy which emerges from such a process involves close co-ordination at the policy level between the main institutions involved in economic policy, particularly the ministry of finance and the central bank. They need not only to define objectives of fiscal, monetary and debt management but to prioritise them according to the situation of the country. They should aim to end up with a plan all of whose aspects are consistent with each other.

2. Assess debt sustainability and need for fiscal adjustment

One of the key assessments policy makers have to make concerns the sustainability of their country's existing stock of debt. There are several theoretical models dealing with this subject. One approach analyses the public sector's balance sheet, listing its assets and liabilities, calculating the present values of future government revenues and expenditures and, on the basis of this, estimating the government's net worth. If it is negative, the debt is unsustainable, and fiscal adjustment necessary. This approach is presented in Appendix I.

ebt sustainability linked ɔ budget deficit, interest rates and growth rates

Another approach raises the issue: would a given fiscal policy result in a stock of domestic debt that is stable? Or would it grow to a level that is insupportable? The key concepts it uses are (a) the stock of debt in proportion to the size of the economy (debt/GDP); (b) the primary deficit, that is fiscal deficit minus that part of expenditure that goes to paying interest on the existing stock of debt; (c) that part of the deficit that can be safely financed by money creation; (d) the inflation-adjusted or real rate of interest on government debt; and (e) the rate of growth of the inflation-adjusted or 'real' GDP.

The theory says that the sustainability of debt is a function of the primary deficit, the real rate of interest, and the growth rate of the economy. Generally speaking, a low growth rate, a high rate of interest and a large primary deficit tend to increase the debt-to-GDP ratio.

Specifically, it says that the debt-to-GDP ratio will be on a rising trend if the real rate of interest exceeds the growth rate unless this is offset by a primary surplus. If the debt-to-GDP ratio is on a rising trend from an initial position that is sustainable, fiscal policy must be adjusted or there will be a crisis. This approach is used to assess the sustainability of fictitious country X's domestic debt in the box on page 18, and a mathematical exposition of the theory is presented in Appendix II.

What this approach makes clear is that debt is never too high in itself, but depends critically on other factors, particularly the growth rate. A debt-to-GDP ratio of, say, 80 per cent, may be unsustainable in a country that is growing relatively slowly, but manageable in a

Box 1: Measuring sustainability: simulation for Country X

Background

In the 1970s, fiscal deficits and public debt did not create much of a problem in Country X, as real interest rates were low and the government could finance the deficit by money creation without much inflation. However, in the 1980s the level of domestic debt in Country X grew rapidly. By 1991–92 interest payments were claiming about half of the central government revenues and inflation was running at 14 per cent. At the same time, Country X's economy got into a balance of payment crisis and it had to embark on an IMF structural adjustment programme. How large a fiscal correction was needed?

Basic formula

The basic formula in the method mentioned above is:

$$db = z - s + b(r - y)$$

Where

b = ratio of debt to GDP

z = ratio of the primary deficit to GDP

s = that part of the deficit that can safely be financed by money creation

r = the real rate of interest on government debt

y = the rate of growth of real GDP

d = symbolises change over a period which in this case is one year.

The formula says the change in the debt ratio is equal to the primary deficit to GDP minus the safe level of seignorage and inflation tax plus the debt ratio multiplied by the real rate of interest on debt minus the real rate of growth.

Applying the formula to Country X's circumstances

In 1991–92, domestic debt of the non-financial public sector was 54 per cent of GDP, so $b = 0.54$

- The primary deficit was 4.4 per cent of GDP, so $z = 0.044$.
- s is an estimate of seignorage and acceptable inflation; a credible estimate is 0.012.
- A credible growth rate of GDP is 5 per cent a year, hence $y = 0.05$.
- Finally, the real rate of interest on debt could be put at 4 per cent, so $r = 0.04$.

Thus:

$$db = 0.044 - 0.012 + 0.54(0.04 - 0.05)$$

or $db = 0.0266$

This means that on these assumptions, the domestic debt ratio will be growing at over 2.5 per cent a year. The terminal value of b can be calculated by setting $db = 0$, and solving for b:

$$b = (z - s) / (y - r)$$

or $b = (0.044 - 0.012) / (0.05 - 0.04) = 3.2$

This means that the domestic debt ratio will end up at 3.2 times GDP. This is clearly unsustainable. Interest charges alone at a 10 per cent nominal interest rate would eat up 32 per cent of GDP!

Adjustment required to achieve sustainability

One can also derive from this method the degree of adjustment needed to make debt sustainable. By making $db = 0$, and $b = 0.54$, we can solve for X to calculate the required reduction in the primary deficit:

$z = s - b(r - y)$, which works out at 0.017.

This means that the primary deficit should be reduced to 1.7 of GDP from 4.4 per cent to keep domestic debt stable.

country that is growing rapidly. That said, it is worth bearing in mind that the future growth rate of an economy is not necessarily independent of the amount of debt its government accumulates. If a country with a relatively large debt but a rapidly growing economy continues to borrow a large proportion of the country's savings, it may affect the growth rate by crowding out private sector investment, and thus make a debt that might have been sustainable, unsustainable.

Prudential rules of thumb and credit risk

Value judgements in ascertaining debt sustainability

The example in the box opposite illustrates an important point: an assessment of debt sustainability cannot carry the certainty of mathematics. One needs to project future tax and expenditure patterns, future inflation and interest rates, and the future economic growth. This necessarily involves a great deal of judgement, and judgement can be fallible.

Nor should one conclude from the proposition that debt that is sustainable is optimal. The best level of debt depends on a number of specific characteristics of the country, such as its people's propensity to save, their tolerance of inflation, how efficiently they employ its capital, its taxable capacity, and, most importantly, the ability of its debt and capital markets to absorb government borrowing. Many developing countries save little; the tolerance of inflation varies considerably; and hardly any have capital markets capable of accommodating large government borrowing.

Rules of thumb to define debt sustainability

Partly because of the inevitable uncertainty in this area, it is prudent to adopt rules of thumb rather than rely on precise calculations. They may seem somewhat arbitrary, but can be of more practical value. This is the approach embodied in the Maastricht Treaty of the European Union. Countries that have signed up to it are required, before they can adopt the common currency, the Euro, to meet certain criteria. Two of them concern debt and deficits: (a) their fiscal deficits should not exceed 3 per cent of GDP, and (b) the gross debt of the government should not exceed 60 per cent of GDP.

Developing countries too should consider adopting similar rules, not just for prudential reasons, but because they are becoming widely used in calculating the credit risk of debt instruments of countries. Here are some rules worth considering:

- Aim to have fiscal deficits below 3 per cent of GDP.
- Public debt service should not exceed 15 per cent of government revenue.

- Public domestic debt should not consistently be higher than 200 per cent of domestically generated government revenue.

Crises, emergency measures and fiscal adjustment

Dangers of financing persistent fiscal deficits

The case for fiscal prudence, therefore, is strong. However, many countries, for a variety of reasons, have found themselves with a level of debt that is unsustainable and have had to endure a crisis. The route to it is well-marked. The problem begins with persistently large deficits. To bridge the gap between spending and revenue, the government resorts to a combination of borrowing abroad (if it can), borrowing from the central bank (printing money), and borrowing from domestic institutions. Since in many developing countries these are government controlled, they borrow from them at below market rates. But as large fiscal deficits persist, this source is not sufficient to plug the gap. So they borrow from others at higher cost, or (more typically) rely more on the central bank. This money creation fuels inflation, which eventually increases the cost of credit. The government may then impose higher statutory ratios on its banks, forcing them to hold a higher and higher amount of its debt. This reduces their profitability and their ability to lend to productive enterprises. The banking system is thus weakened and becomes prone to crisis. If the government can resort to external borrowing, it probably will, but this will eventually result in balance of payments crises and an inability to service its external debt. Finally, there will be a loss of confidence, a flight of capital, and a general crisis in the economy.

How to deal with a debt overhang

Once a crisis is upon a country, it will have to embark on a long term programme to reform its tax and spending policies to reduce its fiscal deficits and bring its debt to a sustainable level. But in the short term it could consider measures to reduce the immediate pressure:

- A combination of external debt reduction and rescheduling to ease budgetary pressure arising out of a persistently high debt service.
- Obtaining quick disbursing grants and concessional borrowing to support the budget.
- Selling public sector assets to the private sector.
- Restructuring debt by issuing securities with longer maturities and change in the terms of domestic debt service.

But such measures are no substitute for reform of government finances. The nature of these reforms falls outside the scope of this compendium, but they are spelt out in detail in several reports of the World Bank and the IMF. Some points are worth noting:

- The sequence of the reforms is important because some of the measures – less reliance on captive borrowing at controlled interest rates, for example – will actually increase the fiscal deficit in the short run.
- The quality of fiscal adjustment is important. The deficit should be cut by increasing public savings rather than by reducing public investment. In particular, the deficit should be reduced without cutting public spending on infrastructure, and on primary education and health, as these are vital for both growth and the alleviation of poverty.

3. Evolve an appropriate borrowing strategy

When policy makers have assessed the sustainability of the government's fiscal stance and decided on the degree of fiscal adjustment required, debt managers need to formulate a credible borrowing strategy. As a first step, they need good forecasts of the borrowing requirement of the government. Then they need to make an assessment of the likely take-up of government securities by the public, the banks and other financial institutions. They should be careful to limit borrowing from the central bank – financing the deficit through money creation. In many countries legal limits and institutional barriers to excessive monetisation have proved useful.

Avoid excessive reliance on short-term debt

In drawing up a schedule of borrowing, debt managers should be careful to avoid an excessive reliance on short-term debt. The schedule should chime in with the redemption dates of maturing loans, the cash needs of the banks and financial institutions and the overall state of liquidity of the economy. It is obvious that this requires close co-ordination with the operation of monetary policy – an issue discussed in more detail below.

Once a schedule of borrowing has been decided, debt managers should be conscious of the benefits of transparency and predictability. Capricious changes to the schedule or unpredictable behaviour by debt managers increases the risk of holding government securities, which in turn ultimately raises their cost of debt to the government.

4. Develop markets for government securities

Properly functioning markets for government securities are necessary both for effective debt management and monetary policy management. For this reason it is important that the authorities – particularly the central bank – take the initiative in developing them. Initially, they will concentrate on developing primary markets for debt securities, and at this stage they are likely to use the same instruments for debt management and monetary control.

Goal is to separate debt management and monetary policy operations

Later the authorities should seek to develop secondary markets in government securities. When this has developed, the operations of debt management and monetary policy can be more easily separated.

At its most undeveloped or primitive stage, there is virtually no market of government debt. The government's deficit is almost entirely financed by the central bank, except that part of it which the government can borrow abroad. There is therefore hardly any domestic debt held outside the central bank. If the government incurs a deficit, it is monetised. This is an inherently inflationary situation.

Some of the debt then tends to be sold by the central banks to commercial banks. They are obliged to hold a proportion of their assets in the form of government securities. The interest they earn on it is set by fiat of the central bank – it bears little relation to the market and is usually low. These banks are in effect captive lenders to the government. They tend to hold the securities to maturity and there is little trading. Other financial institutions, usually state-owned pension funds or insurance companies, are sometimes also obliged to hold government debt. As one would expect, at this stage, money markets are weak and the interbank markets thin.

Creating a market for government securities

The first step in moving from this situation involves the creation of a market for short-term government securities, usually Treasury bills, the idea being that a market for longer term securities can be created later. The creation of a Treasury bill market can be a powerful spur to the development of money markets by encouraging banks to manage their liquidity more actively. At the outset, the authorities should decide whether the primary market for Treasury bills should be used strictly to finance the fiscal deficit or also be a tool for monetary management.

Before the development of secondary markets in Treasury bills, some countries have used primary issues of Treasury bills at auctions to regulate bank reserves. This is a step towards fully-fledged indirect monetary management through open-market operations (OMOs) and is called open-market-type operations. As explained in the box on page 24, indirect monetary management involves targeting bank reserves to control their lending capacity, and short-term interest rates to determine the broad structure of interest rates.

It is possible to do this before secondary trading in Treasury bills has developed, but it is difficult. These auctions need to be held frequently and at market-clearing interest rates, so that the volume of these sales can determine bank reserves and the interest rates set the general interest rates structure in the economy. In practice, it is not likely that these auctions will be sufficiently flexible to enable the authorities to control sudden feasts and famines of liquidity. Therefore, there is a need for refinance/rediscount or repurchase agreements (Repos) which the authorities can use to increase or decrease liquidity for short periods. In addition, the central bank, purely for monetary management purposes, may employ other tools to supplement Treasury bills, in particular:

- **Central bank securities**: These are bills issued at the discretion of the central bank. They pose the danger of overlapping with Treasury bills. One way out is to issue central bank bills at shorter maturities – say, up to three months – and Treasury bills for longer. Although this might minimise competition between the two instruments, such a segmentation might retard the development of the secondary markets.
- **Central bank credit auctions**: These can be another way in which the central bank can regulate bank reserves. In undeveloped markets commercial banks tend to be heavily dependent on the central bank, and by varying the amount of credit it auctions and letting the interest rate be determined freely, the central bank can use these auctions as a powerful monetary tool. In such circumstances, Treasury bills could be used largely as a means of funding rather than for monetary policy.
- **Government deposits**: Some countries transfer government deposit balances between the central bank and commercial banks as another means of influencing the banks' reserves and conditions in the money markets.

Treasury bill auctions – need for competitive bidding and transparent mechanisms

It is important to ensure that the Treasury bill auctions as far as possible conform to the criteria of free markets, in particular, that prices are determined by competitive bidding, that the auction mechanism is transparent and that there is a regular and well-publicised calendar to which the central bank adheres. There are two other questions which should be addressed:

- **Should participation in the auctions be restricted?** In many countries only certain types of institutions are allowed to bid, and in some there are further restrictions arising from the requirement that some bidders can enter the auction only through the agency of banks. There may be good practical reasons for this, but it is important to ensure that the risk of collusion between bidders is minimised. In some countries participation is restricted to a group of authorised institutions called primary dealers. But this arrangement is justified only in so far that this exclusive privilege is matched by obligations on primary dealers to act as secondary market makers. This is discussed later.

- **Should the central bank itself participate in auctions?** In general, this is undesirable, but if it is necessary because the market cannot absorb the issues, the central bank should be careful to participate in a way that does not put itself into competition with other bidders.

Box 2: The operation of monetary policy

Monetary policy involves the use by the central bank of certain instruments to determine short-term interest rates and bank reserves in order to control inflation and maintain a stable and adequate level of liquidity in the economy. Until recently, central banks of developing countries used direct instruments: credit controls, interest rate ceilings, statutory liquidity ratios (whereby banks have to place a certain proportion of their deposits in government assets), and directed credit programmes.

In the past few years it has become generally accepted that the economy works better if central banks exercise monetary control through financial markets. This involves indirect methods of control: open market operations (OMOs), reserve requirements and discount operations. Open market operations are the sale or purchase of financial instruments such as Treasury bills. The central bank can also use repurchase agreements (Repos) – purchase securities under contract to resell them at a specified price on a given date – or reverse repurchase agreements. These are used to increase or decrease bank reserves. Rediscounting facilities are a way for the central bank to lend money through rediscounting government securities. Reserve requirements oblige banks to hold a specified part of their deposits in the central bank, usually at nil interest.

Many Commonwealth developing countries are in transition in monetary management from direct controls to indirect controls. The move to indirect controls necessitates the development of markets for government securities. The task for many is complicated by the legacy of having to cope with a monetary overhang – excess liquidity that has resulted from financing large and persistent fiscal deficits by borrowing from the central bank, in other words, by printing money. To reduce the inflationary potential of this, the central bank needs to mop it up. But this is far from a costless process. If it does so through issuing Treasury securities, it will increase the debt of the government and hence the cost of servicing it. If it mops up the excess by issuing its own securities, its own profits would be reduced, and the cost of this will eventually be borne by the government, by way of fewer profits to this consolidated fund.

This tension between putting monetary policy on to a sound footing and keeping down the cost of debt runs right through many of the measures involved in moving to a market-based system of monetary control. These include:

- stopping ad hoc government borrowing from the central bank and reducing the share of central bank financing of government deficits in favour of non-inflationary sources;
- developing an active money market;
- developing a Treasury bill market where the central bank can conduct its OMOs;
- removing direct controls on interest rates and credit allocation;
- promoting a competitive and strong financial sector;
- setting up markets for secondary trading in government securities.

Deregulating interest rates and strengthening banks

Well-functioning financial markets require a sound and independent banking sector in which managers are actively engaged in managing their assets to increase the strength and profitability of their portfolios. Most Commonwealth developing countries which have embarked on the process of reform begin with a legacy of a crippled banking sector in which:

- banks are owned or controlled by the state – their management has a civil service not a commercial culture;
- banks are forced to lend a large part of their loanable resources to the government and a significant part to sectors deemed socially worthy or to other government-owned enterprises that are failing;
- lending rates are set by the government.

Unsurprisingly, many banks are entering a market-oriented environment crippled by a portfolio of non-performing loans.

Banking reform as part of overall financial sector reform

It is vital to reform the banking sector as part of an overall strategy to reform the financial sector. This involves moves to strengthen the banks' portfolio and capital base and to reduce and ultimately eliminate government direction of credit allocation and interest rates. But these moves must be underpinned by a prudential framework for bank regulation and supervision. Preparation of new banking legislation, conferring greater supervisory powers to central banks and ensuring that banks comply with the regulations, is essential for success.

Developing secondary markets

Secondary markets necessary for debt management and monetary control

As remarked earlier, secondary markets for government securities are necessary to achieve the aims of debt management and for indirect monetary control. In particular, secondary markets:

- help fix the terms of new issues;
- reduce the risk for investors by providing them with a mechanism for selling the securities for which they are bidding;
- are an essential prop for the creation of market interest rate structures, thus allowing genuine open market operations for monetary policy;
- encourage the development of new products such as options and futures based on government securities; and
- provide benchmark interest rates for corporate bonds.

Experience has shown that well-functioning secondary markets – that is, those in which a broad spectrum of investors participate and in which they can trade easily when they choose – for government securities do not develop without the help of the authorities, particularly the central bank. Therefore they should take a number of initiatives:

Need for reliable payments, clearing and settlement system

- They need to create a framework of regulation and supervision. To accomplish this, some have created a securities commission, a central body which looks after all aspects in this area. Governments also need to remove from existing laws any burdens on issuing and trading government securities. New legislation may be needed to introduce scripless securities if paperless transactions are thought desirable.

Market makers can facilitate trading in securities

- The business of buying and selling stock can be hugely facilitated by market makers, principals who provide two-way prices whenever the market is open and are prepared to deal at them. This can be a risky business, and market makers may need certain privileges that compensate them for the risk. The central bank can help by authorising a group of market makers as primary dealers, giving them specified privileges in return for specified obligations. The privileges could include an exclusive access to the auctions of government securities or some other advantages, for example, no prepayment requirements, telephone or electronic bidding, options on additional purchases of stock at non-competitive prices. In some countries market makers have access to privileged information, in others they receive favourable tax treatment, or rights to borrow securities or take short positions. In return for these privileges, primary dealers are obliged to make continuous two-way prices in government securities.

Essential role of primary dealers in secondary markets

Primary dealers can play a vital role in the development of secondary markets. By holding inventories of securities, they help keep prices stable. Because they stand in the centre of the market, they can incorporate all the available information into the prices they quote, thus making markets efficient. By taking positions, they offer immediacy of execution to market participants. Finally, they help educate investors in the characteristics of securities and the advantages of holding or trading them.

Primary dealers can also provide valuable assistance to the central bank by keeping it informed of the latest market developments and the state of demand, and assisting it in designing new instruments. In considering the privileges to offer in return for the services primary dealers render, central banks should consider both the present stage of market development and the future. Some privileges may assist growth in the present but inhibit it in the future. Thus some privileges should be granted on a temporary basis. Central banks also need to be able to trust dealers and to supervise them.

Box 3: The role of the Central Bank in the development of debt securities markets in Sri Lanka

The limited maturity structure of market instruments, the absence of market making systems and regulatory constraints deterred the development of an active secondary market in Treasury bills in Sri Lanka and this, in turn, hindered the development of the market for long-term securities. The Central Bank initiated a number of improvements which transformed the situation. In 1992, it appointed a group of approved primary dealers (APDs) consisting of 14 bank and 4 non-bank primary dealers. The number has now been increased to 21, comprising 15 banks and 6 non-banks, which were expected to develop secondary markets for Treasury bills and government securities. As part of the on-going financial sector reform, the Central Bank also strengthened its involvement by amending a series of legislation and streamlining activities to support the development of the debt securities market. The changes it initiated include:

(i) Amendments to the Monetary Law Act; the Credit Information Bureau Act; the National Savings Bank Act; the National Development Bank Act; the Development Finance Corporation of Ceylon Act; the State Mortgage and Investment Bank Act; the Registered Stocks and Securities Ordinance (RSSO); the Local Treasury Bills Ordinance; and the introduction of a new section to the RSSO to deal with Scripless Securities. These amendments enabled the Central Bank to auction and trade in Treasury bills and government securities and to further strengthen the financial sector.

(ii) Varying the maturity structure of debt instruments and removal of administrative and regulatory constraints relating to the issue of debt securities.

(iii) Issue of guidelines to Approved Primary Dealers setting out their privileges and responsibilities in market making and streamlining of their operations.

(iv) Closure of the Central Bank's secondary Treasury bills window, which provided short-term funds exclusively to commercial banks and selected non-bank institutions, and the opening of the Repo Window to all market dealers.

(v) Publication of the maturity structure of Treasury bills on a weekly basis and the issue of long-dated Treasury bonds with different maturities.

(vi) Issue of investment guidelines to the largest long-term fund holding agency, the Employees Provident Fund, enabling it to diversify portfolio investments by permitting it to invest 5–10% of its inflow of funds in securities other than government securities.

(vii) Selection of a core group of potential fund managers from contractual savings organisations (EPF, ETF and Insurance Companies) and providing practical training to them on fund management.

(viii) Introduction of the Reverse Repo Facility in November 1995 to stabilise call money market interest rates and to intensify open market operations.

(ix) Provision of extensive testing facilities and training for computerised trading programmes coupled with visits to other central banks which have sophisticated trading facilities.

(x) Withdrawal, with effect from June 1994, of the withholding tax placed on interest on domestic debt instruments to encourage market players to develop secondary trading in government debt.

(xi) Permission for commercial banks to obtain foreign loans up to 5% of their capital and reserves.

(xii) Amendments to the National Savings Bank Act providing a capital base and making its operations more market oriented.

(xiii) Permission for non-Board of Investment exporters to obtain foreign currency loans through domestic units and offshore units of commercial banks.

(xiv) Commencement of Treasury Bond Auctions.

Source: Central Bank of Sri Lanka

- A reliable payments, clearing and settlements system is an essential feature of a good secondary market. Central banks should encourage banks or other institutions to develop these industries in their countries or provide the services themselves. There are four elements involved when a security is traded: (a) the trade has to be cleared, (b) ownership has to be transferred, usually by a depository, (c) the money has to be transferred, and (d) the security has to be kept safely by a custodian. What is important is that the transfer of the security by the depository and opposite movement of funds should be done simultaneously in a way that ensures 'delivery versus payment'.

The central bank may also need to take the initiative in training. When secondary markets in government securities get going, it will often be the case that there is a shortage of the skills necessary to run such a market. So the central bank may need to establish training programmes in securities trading for potential market participants, and for its own personnel and those from the Treasury, in monetary and debt management.

When secondary market trading in short-term government securities becomes established, the central bank should encourage such trading in instruments with longer maturities. This will involve the participation of pension and insurance funds who typically need such long-term securities because their liabilities are long term. In many countries such institutions suffer from the same institutional atrophy as do the banks, and reforms aimed at making them more efficient will be necessary.

5. Improve co-ordination between debt and monetary management

Clear allocation of responsibilities between ministries of finance and central banks

Effective debt management requires close co-ordination between the ministry of finance and the central bank, particularly in the early stages of market development, when debt management is closely tied to monetary management. In most developing countries co-ordination is weak. There is often no clear allocation of responsibilities, no sharing of vital information, procedures for implementing policies are undefined and meetings of key committees are irregular. Strengthening institutional co-ordination should be given high priority.

There should be clear and transparent procedures for taking decisions and implementing them. As a general rule, the ministry of finance is responsible for the size of the fiscal deficit and the broad parameters of the government's borrowing programme, and the public debt office for raising funds, managing the issue structure, retiring or renewing existing debt that falls due. Because of the close links with monetary policy, the public debt office is often located in

Box 4: Tanzania's key steps relating to government domestic debt operations

The Economic Recovery Programme (ERP), begun in 1986, aims to improve macro-economic management, address the underlying structural weaknesses and encourage more active private sector participation. The programme involves policies to increase output, reduce inflation and improve the balance of payments. Integral to this process are the liberalisation of domestic markets and improving debt management, both domestic and external. Presented below are events that have relevance to monetary policy, fiscal policy and debt management:

1993

Jan	Issuance of Bank of Tanzania (BOT) certificates of deposit as part of a contractionary monetary policy.
July	The BOT removed the maximum lending rate of 31% for commercial banks as a step liberalisation of interest rates.
Aug	The BOT commenced Treasury Bill Auctions with 91-day Bills as a tool for financing short-term government debt, an instrument of liquidity management and as a reference point for the determining of market interest rates.
Sep	35-day Treasury Bill introduced for Treasury Bill auctions.

1994

Jan	The Capital and Securities Act enacted.
Jan	The Discount Rate, the rate at which BOT accommodates commercial banks on short-term basis, was increased from 27% to 50% per annum. Thereafter the rate was to be adjusted bi-weekly, on the basis of marginal yields in the auction of the 91-day Treasury Bill.
Feb	The 182-day Treasury Bill was introduced in the Treasury Bill Market.
Aug	The minimum interest rate on 12-month fixed deposits was abolished. Before, the rate was positive in real terms.
Sep	Vault cash was included in determining the Minimum Reserve Requirements in addition to all deposit liabilities, excluding foreign currency deposits.
Oct	The calculation of the Discount Rate was determined on the basis of the weighted average of T-Bill Auction yields for all maturities.
Dec	The 35-day Treasury Bills were discontinued from the auctions.

1995

Mar	The Capital Market and Securities Exchange was inaugurated by the Finance Minister.
July	The Bank of Tanzania Act (1995) became effective, empowering the BOT with a single policy objective of price stability.
Aug	All banks and financial institutions were required to publish quarterly financial statements and audited financial statements in newspapers that circulate widely in Tanzania. Liquid assets ratio was abolished.

1996

Jan	The government adopted cash budget system to control inflationary spending and reduce the budget deficit.
Apr	The entitlement of commercial banks to hold up to 50% of their Statutory Minimum Reserve in Treasury Bills was abolished.
July	The Tanzania Revenue Authority (TRA) was established in a bid to improve tax administration. Credit ceiling on commercial bank lending was abolished.

1997

Apr	New Banking and Financial Institutions Regulations were gazetted.

Source: Bank of Tanzania

the central bank, but sometimes certain aspects of even short-term debt management remain in the ministry of finance. In countries where markets are advanced and monetary management can be completely separated from debt management, the public debt office can be made independent of both the central bank and the ministry of finance. But this is not possible in developing countries. For them, the merits or otherwise of an independent debt office are a theoretical matter, albeit one which may become important in the future.

Need for debt and monetary policy co-ordination

Given the close relationship between public debt management and monetary policy, there is a strong argument for establishing a joint monetary and debt management co-ordination committee consisting of senior officials from central bank and the ministry of finance. This would set targets for the sale of government securities in the light of the government's borrowing requirement and targets for inflation, and see that appropriate policies are implemented. It could also guide the development of the markets for government securities and co-ordinate policy links between external and domestic debt management. A stylised representation of the institutional arrangement for monetary and debt management is shown in the diagram opposite.

Need for central bank autonomy

Close co-ordination between the central bank and the ministry of finance is essential, but it is equally important that central banks do not become arms of the government. As a long-term goal they should become independent of the ministry, but even in the short term they should acquire a fair degree of autonomy. As a step in this direction, the government could put a limit on the automatic financing of the government's cash needs from the central bank.

6. Improve debt data management

Effective debt management requires comprehensive and up-to-date databases. Public debt needs to be categorised into borrowers (central government, state governments, public sector enterprises and other decentralised agencies); by debt instruments (marketable and non-marketable); by maturities (short and long-term) and interest structure (fixed and floating). The information system should have the capacity to generate borrowing trends, redemption schedules, interest payments, and to make projections based on planned transactions.

Computerisation of debt data essential for efficient debt operations and analysis

Since the database is large, computers can be useful for debt accounting and statistical reporting. They are also helpful in preparing reports and supporting managerial functions. A computer-based debt management information system can be used for storing information related to debt management, retrieving and organising information reports, carrying out debt analyses and relating debt

Structure of institutional arrangements for monetary and debt management

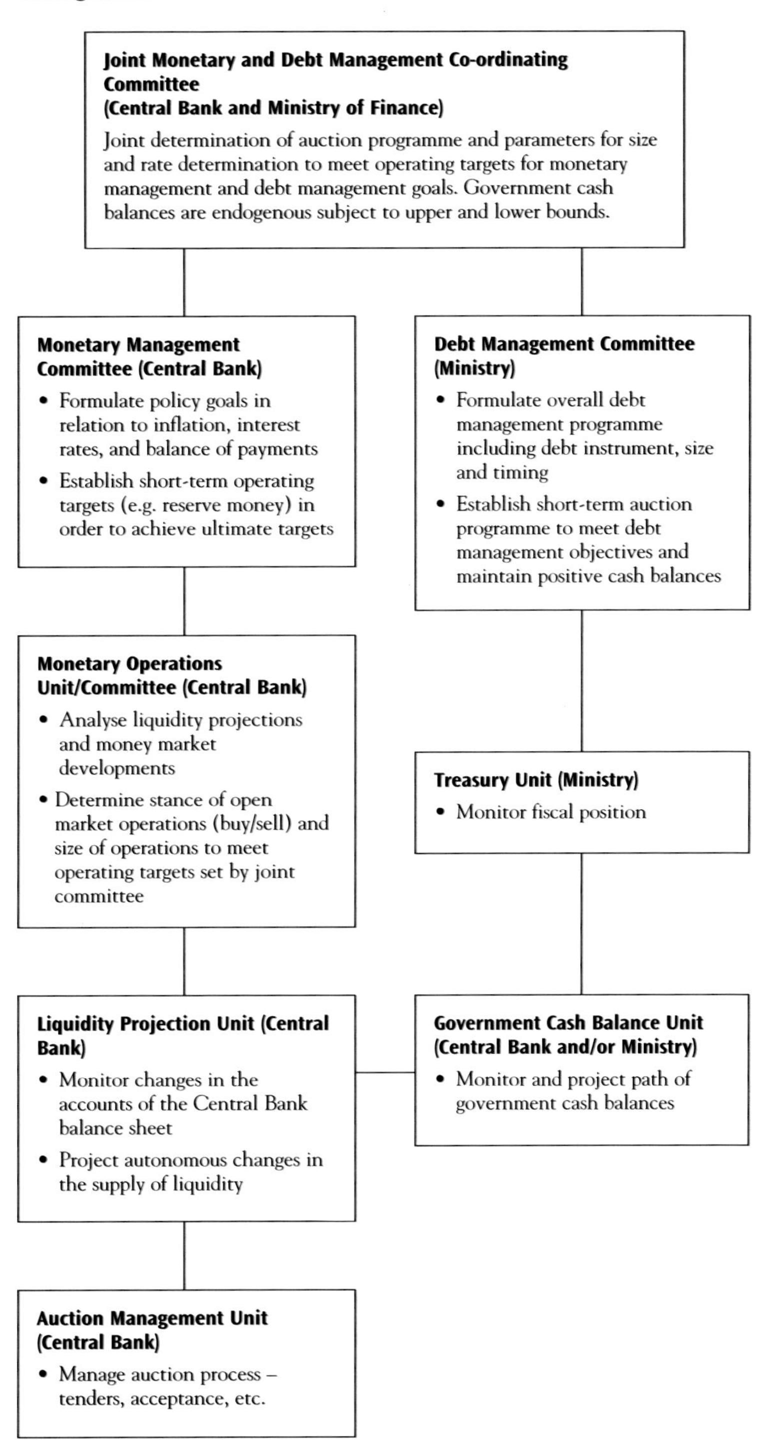

Source: IMF

information to other data systems. The system should be able to produce standard reports as well as querying and ad hoc reporting. The system should be able to provide analytical support tools to facilitate policy and strategy formulation.

Commonwealth Secretariat programme of assistance in debt and development resource management

The Commonwealth Secretariat has an integrated programme of assistance in various areas of debt management for its 54 member countries. The programme which was formally launched in 1985, is handled by the Secretariat's Economic and Legal Advisory Services Division. The advisory services cover the following areas:

- Strengthening legal and institutional arrangements for contracting and managing debt.
- Provision of the in-house developed computer software – Commonwealth Secretariat Debt Recording and Management System (CS-DRMS).
- Assisting in the data compilation and recording as well as reviewing the quality of debt databases.
- Capacity-building through training courses and workshops on various issues of debt management as well as on the use of CS-DRMS.
- Providing direct advice to member countries in areas such as debt restructuring, debt strategy and evaluating various loan offers, including negotiating with creditors.
- Providing debt experts on long-term assignment in member countries.

CS-DRMS is more than a computer software – it is a model of best practice in debt management. CS-DRMS enables countries to capture both external and domestic borrowing, and can also handle grants and government lending. It has the potential to analyse borrowing and lending operations in an integrated manner. It assists ministers of finance and central banks in forecasting and budgeting debt service payments, monitoring disbursements, evaluating new borrowing and planning reserves. The system has electronic links with the World Bank's debtor reporting system as well as with the Debt Sustainability Model-Plus (DSM+) of the World Bank. There is a facility to export information into spreadsheets such as Excel for further manipulation.

The software is regularly updated to take account of changes in creditor practices, market instruments, user requirements and computer technology. CS-DRMS runs both in English and French, and has facilities to accommodate other languages. The CS-DRMS software is currently undergoing a three-year modernisation programme, with many new features, including expanded facilities for debt analysis, new modules focusing on government on-lending, the increasingly important area of domestic debt, and improved access for a larger number of users with differing needs. Phase One of the modernisation was completed in 1997 with the release of Version 7.1, which features a new, more user-friendly display, including Windows interface. The new version, CS-DRMS 2000+ is scheduled for release in late 2000.

The *CS-DRMS Newsletter*, produced twice a year, describes the activities of the Commonwealth Secretariat in debt management.

Some 2,000 staff from member countries have been trained in various areas of debt management and CS-DRMS. Training has covered topics such as the interpretation of loan agreements, debt data capture and analysis, debt strategies and techniques, debt sustainability analysis and effective domestic debt management.

Box 5: Domestic debt module in CS-DRMS

Over the years, the Economic and Legal Advisory Services Division (ELASD) of the Commonwealth Secretariat has made considerable efforts to improve debt management capacity in member countries. The programme of assistance comprises policy advice for debt management and technical assistance through the provision of the in-house developed Commonwealth Secretariat Debt Recording and Management System (CS-DRMS) software, which includes both external and domestic debt modules. The software has become a model of good practices in debt management and is in use in over 70 sites in 49 countries, including 7 outside the Commonwealth.

The domestic debt module in the system allows users/countries to record various instruments of domestic borrowing: Standard Loans, Treasury Bills, Treasury Bonds, Government Stocks and Savings and Deposit Certificates. The system is able to generate forecasts of debt service, monitor arrears and assist in guiding debt policies including borrowing strategies. The software provides useful domestic debt reports to guide economic managers in decision making. Over the years, however, there have been major developments in domestic debt markets encompassing: a new range of debt instruments, including those specifically to target different types of investors – retailers and wholesale, instruments to diversify the maturity structure of domestic debt and facilities to promote secondary trading of debt instruments. As markets become sophisticated, new systems need to be introduced that can assist in formulating dynamic benchmark debt portfolios, transforming them through numerous debt management techniques. Towards this end, the CS-DRMS is being modernised. CS-DRMS 2000+ which is scheduled for release in late 2000, will greatly enhance functionality in the area of domestic debt management.

3. Checklist for Action

The Economic and Legal Advisory Services Division (ELAS) of the Commonwealth Secretariat held three workshops on Effective Domestic Debt Management in June 1996 for the Caribbean region, in December 1996 for countries from the Asia–Pacific region, and in March 1998 for African countries. At the end of each workshop an action plan based on the discussions was issued to all participating countries. A checklist of the action plan is presented below, and reflects the areas where further consideration is required on domestic debt matters.

1. Debt management objectives

- Consider domestic debt operations in the context of the economic conditions prevailing in your country.
- Define the objectives of domestic debt management.
- Prioritise them according to your country's needs.
- Define the role of debt managers and encourage them to promote the objectives of debt management.

2. Fiscal management

- Improve revenue sources through tax reform.
- Undertake expenditure and administrative reforms and correct fiscal imbalances through fiscal restraints.
- Analyse sustainability of debt, maintain debt servicing at manageable levels and conduct periodic review of interest rates on debt instruments.
- Review borrowing limits, analyse outstanding debt levels and streamline government cash flow operations, restore public confidence in government debt operations.

3. Policy co-ordination

- Harmonise fiscal and monetary policies.
- Agree on common goals involved in fiscal, monetary and debt management.

- Reduce or eliminate government intervention in the operation of markets, but introduce regulatory and supervisory systems to ensure their orderly development and the protection of investors.

4. *Deficit financing*

- Analyse merits and demerits of borrowing through various instruments.
- Advise debt managers, where possible, to engage in least cost methods of borrowing.
- Avoid monetary financing.
- Establish overall government borrowing ceilings.
- Introduce legislation or amend existing legislation to incorporate government borrowing ceilings (if such statutory ceilings do not exist).
- Avoid borrowing for long-term purposes through the issue of short-term debt instruments.
- Review financial positions of sinking funds (if any) and improve their ability to redeem debt by allowing them to invest in high return investments.

5. *Development of debt securities markets*

- Central banks to initiate action to develop domestic or regional markets for debt securities.
- Individual countries to ensure that necessary preconditions are established to set up regional debt markets.
- Appoint a reputable and well-capitalised group of institutions for market making.
- Prepare guidelines for market makers, outlining their privileges and responsibilities.
- Deregulate markets by removing administrative controls on interest rates and barriers to entry for investors.
- Design and install systems for cheque payment, clearing, settlement and trading systems for debt securities.
- Remove tax, legislative, regulatory and institutional and other administrative constraints on the sale, trading and investment in debt securities.
- Improve primary Treasury bills market and encourage active trading in the secondary market.
- Allow captive institutions to manage their portfolios professionally.

- Begin open market operations by central banks.
- Begin issuing debt securities with different maturity structures and in a sequential order to ensure regular supply of debt instruments to the market.
- Promote the issuing and trading of private debt securities.
- Enhance the role of the central banks in effective debt management and delegate responsibilities to debt managers.
- Issue development bonds for financing of projects.
- Establish training programmes for staff of the central banks, ministries of finance, and contractual savings organisations (captive funds), on domestic debt management, portfolio management, debt issues and selling techniques.

6. *Contingent liabilities and parastatal debt*

- Establish an effective system of debt operations of parastatals and public enterprises.
- Introduce limits on overdraft facilities given to parastatals and public enterprises.
- Privatise (fully or in part) public enterprises which are dependant on budgetary resources.
- Review criteria for providing government guarantees.

7. *Institutional arrangements and operational co-ordination*

- Set up an appropriate institutional structure, including debt review committees to ensure co-ordination of fiscal, monetary and debt management operations.
- Establish close co-ordination among debt management units in the ministry of finance, the central bank and the accountant general's department.

8. *Data collection, recording and computerisation*

- Debt management unit to collect, record, analyse information relating to domestic debt and submit periodic reports to senior staff, policy makers and co-ordination committees.
- Use computer-assisted data recording and management systems, such as CS-DRMS.
- Provide adequate incentives – involving salaries, training and promotion – to staff in debt management units.

Appendix 1: An Analytical Framework for Fiscal Policy and Public Debt

Balance sheet of public sector

Government assets can be thought of as being composed of two parts: the first is the current stock of assets (the conventional definition); the second is the present value of anticipated future revenues from tax and non-tax sources. Current assets include both domestic and foreign assets. The present value of future revenues is the expected stream of revenues discounted back to the present using a given discount rate. Thus, revenues expected in the future can be analysed in terms of current assets. The notion of present value is important, because it underscores a fundamental equivalence between the stock and the flow dimensions of fiscal policy: that is, it makes it clear that revenues expected in the future are as relevant in determining a government's ability to meet its liabilities as current revenues.

Similarly, corresponding to government assets, government liabilities can also be thought of as composed of two parts: (1) the current outstanding stock of debt and other current obligations (the conventional definition), and (2) the present value of future expenditures, including subsidies. This way of looking at government assets and liabilities is useful, because the determinants of both short-term and long-term fiscal performance are integrated into a single forward-looking balance sheet.

The difference between the government's assets and liabilities is its net worth. On the one hand, if assets exceeded liabilities, then net worth is positive and the government is regarded as being solvent – that is, it is able to meet both its current and future obligations. On the other hand, if net worth is negative, then the government is insolvent and, without an increase in its assets, it is not able to meet its current contractual debt obligations. Therefore, in the ensuing discussion, it is assumed that the flow of government revenues from taxes and other sources constitutes the main source of funds available to service public debt. The issue of public sector solvency is of particular importance when one is dealing with highly indebted countries, and it will be examined at length below.

The implications of the above framework can be seen clearly by using the following identity, which schematically presents a government's balance sheet in terms of domestic currency:

$$EA^* + R = G + S + B + EB^* + K$$

where G, S, and R denote the present values of (expected) government expenditures, subsidies, and (tax and non-tax) revenues; A^* denotes the stock of foreign exchange reserves; B and B^* denote domestic and external government debt, respectively. E denotes the exchange rate. By assumption, B is denominated in local currency while A^* and B^* are denominated in foreign currency. K denotes the government's net worth. Consequently, government assets appear on the left-hand side of its balance sheet while government liabilities appear on the right-hand side. Because the balance sheet focuses only on those assets which are considered most likely to be used to service the public debt, K provides a measure of the government's net worth which is relevant in assessing the public sector's ability to service its liabilities. Therefore, it is important to stress that for the purposes of the discussion below, solvency is defined only with respect to this notion of government net worth.

Implications of the balance-sheet approach

The forward-looking balance sheet provides several interesting insights. First, for a given net worth to be maintained, any increase in debt has to be matched by one or both of the following: (1) an increase in government revenues or current assets; and (2) a decrease in expenditures. The changes in revenues and/or expenditures refer to their present values and, hence, comprise not only current fiscal adjustments but also any expectations of future improvements.

Second, domestic and external debt appear to enter the statement of public sector liabilities on an equal footing – that is, domestic and external debt have equal claims on government resources. Therefore, if an external debt-servicing problem exists, it is likely that a domestic debt-servicing problem also exists. This simple observation suggests that departures from the equivalence of claims should be based on a recognition that the characteristics of the two types of debt may be quite different and that, as a result, government policies for managing the two types of debt may also differ significantly.

From the above observations, it follows that domestic debt problems may occur where the ratio of domestic debt to GDP is low by international standards if, at the same time, either the ratio of external debt to GDP is high or the current or expected future fiscal position is weak.

Third, the present value of the anticipated future stream of government expenditure and subsidies is also a form of government debt to the extent that the stream is perceived as a permanent obligation. This equivalence appears to be particularly relevant for subsidies and transfers, because they may be thought of as representing promises to provide flows of payments in much the same way governments agree to make contractual interest payments. By the same token, the stream of future taxes can be regarded as a form of government asset. For this reason, solving the debt problem may involve, for example, a cut in subsidies or an increase in taxes. In this sense, a reduction in subsidies represents a reduction of government liabilities just as a reduction in debt would.

An illustration of the equivalence between debt and the discounted present value of government expenditures and subsidies is provided by remuneration paid on bank reserves – a government transfer quite often employed in developing countries. Paying interest on reserves held against bank deposits is an interesting example, because whether such payments are included in government expenditure or are considered to be interest on part of the domestic debt depends on the government's accounting practices. On the one hand, a straight transfer would take place if the central bank just paid remuneration on commercial banks' reserves without acknowledging the latter as part of its domestic debt. On the other hand, some countries (for example, Argentina until recently) consider part of these reserves to be government obligations. In this situation, the central bank's transfer would become an interest payment.

Finally, it follows from the forward-looking balance sheet that whether a government is solvent or not depends on the amount of its expenditures (including subsidies), its total revenues, and its debt. On the one hand, a government is solvent if its net worth is not negative, or, to put it differently, a solvent government does not have a debt problem. On the other hand, if a government's net worth is negative, it will not be able to service fully its debt obligations.

What happens when a government is insolvent or nearly insolvent? Consider first the case where total contractual debt has reached the maximum level that can be serviced and therefore, the government's net worth is zero. If solvency is to be maintained, there cannot be any further increase in liabilities without a corresponding increase in assets. Thus, any increase in domestic debt not matched by an equivalent increase in assets should be met either by a decrease in the contractual value of external debt (for instance, by debt relief) or by a decrease in the present discounted value of expenditures and subsidies. Otherwise, the government will become insolvent.

A government's insolvency has two main implications. First, if the government has no other assets to draw on in order to cover a negative net worth, the market value of its contractual obligations will have to fall; the market value, then, reflects the government's perceived debt-servicing capacity. The market value can only fall if domestic and external debt trade at less than their contractual values – that is, if they trade at a discount. In fact, those discounts will be set by the market at levels where a government's net worth will not be negative. Recalling the forward-looking balance sheet, this implies that

$$EA^* + R = G + S + qB + Eq^*B^*$$

where the prices of domestic debt and foreign debt, which are denoted by q and q^*, respectively, are less than unity, so that the discounts are $1 - q$ and $1 - q^*$, respectively.

While the market value of total debt (i.e., $qB + Eq^* B^*$) has to decline when there is the perception of insolvency, the shares of the burden that fall on domestic and foreign debt can differ markedly if the characteristics of the two debts are different. For example, if domestic debt were perceived as having, in some sense, seniority over external debt, q might not fall; hence, the brunt of the adjustment would be borne by the market price of external debt, q^*

The second implication of government insolvency concerns the issuance of new debt. If an insolvent government is able to issue new domestic debt without a corresponding improvement in its debt-servicing ability (e.g. by increasing assets or by strengthening its primary fiscal stance), then any new debt issues are likely to induce capital losses on previous creditors by depressing even more the market value of outstanding debt. The question then becomes, how can this debt be issued?

One possible explanation is that the domestic debt provides liquidity services to its holders. Such would be the case, for example, if banks were allowed to hold new debt as part of their legal reserves against bank deposits. New debt could then be taken up even if its market value were less than its contractual value. This is similar to the case in which the banking system is forced to hold debt at interest rates lower than market rates. The issuance of debt is feasible because it is likely to result in lower rates being paid on bank deposits, which continue to be held voluntarily by the public because of their superior liquidity relative to other financial assets.

Even if new debt did not provide liquidity services to the holder, it might still be issued if its yield were high enough to compensate bondholders for the anticipated capital loss owing to government insolvency. A third possibility is that the new domestic debt might be issued if it were perceived by the public as being 'senior' relative to external debt – in other words, if holders of domestic debt believed that whatever government resources were available would be used to service their debt first. Such a perception could reflect a belief that the costs associated with default are substantially higher when the holders of government paper are domestic residents. The public perception of the seniority of domestic debt compared with external debt, however, is likely to vanish rapidly if the government faces problems in servicing its domestic debt.

Appendix II: Conditions for Debt Sustainability

This is a simplified framework of debt sustainability based on the work of Blanchard. It explains when a debt situation becomes explosive and fiscal deficits are unsustainable. A fiscal plan can be considered sustainable, if, together with a plausible set of assumptions about the key macro-economic variables, it results in a terminal value of debt-to-GDP ratio that is equal to the initial ratio. This initial ratio corresponds to a year when fiscal policy was sustainable, with an acceptable rate of inflation. The target variable is the debt-to-GDP ratio, a measure of the debt relative to the size of the economy. The following notations are used:

B = Nominal stock of debt

I = Nominal interest rate

P = Price level

p = Inflation rate (i.e. percentage change in P)

r = Real interest rate (i.e. I – p)

Y = Level of real output

y = Growth rate of output

z = Primary deficit

b = Debt to income ratio (i.e. B/PY)

S = Monetary base measured as currency plus non-interest bearing deposits

The budget identity of the central government can be written as follows:

(1) $Z + iB = dS + dB$

where d stands for change over one period.

Equation (1) states that the sum total of primary deficit (z) and interest payments on existing debt (iB) should be financed by increase in monetary base (dS, which is seignorage) and increase in government borrowing (dB). Dividing both sides of equation (1) by the GDP (i.e. PY), the following can be derived:

(2) $z + ib = s + dB/PY$

The lower case letters indicate the proportions of GDP. Since b = B/PY, we can derive for the change in B (i.e. dB), by using simple fraction rule of calculus, as follows:

(3) $dB = PYdb + bPY(dP/P + dY/Y)$

or

(4) $dB = PYdb + bPY(p + y)$

or

$$(5) \qquad dB/PY = db + b(p + y)$$

Replacing (5) in (2) and rearranging the term, db can be derived as:

$$(6) \qquad db = (z - s) + b(r - y), \text{ since } r - I - p$$

Equation (6) explains the change in debt-to-income ratio (db) through four components: primary deficit to GDP ratio (z), financing of deficits by base money (s), the growth rate of GDP (y) and the real interest rate (r). Setting db = 0, that is, no change in debt-GDP ratio in the limiting case, we can solve for b as follows:

$$(7) \qquad b = (z - s) / (y - r)$$

Appendix III: Some Recent Contributions to the Academic Literature on Debt Management

There is increasing research interest in issues relating to domestic debt management. For example, Dornbusch and Draghi (1990) contains ten papers and discussion, on the management of public debt and its implications for financial stability. Contributions focus on the efficient design of public debt; indexation and maturity of government bonds; public confidence and debt management; confidence crises and public debt management; funding crises in the aftermath of World War I; the capital levy in theory and practice; episodes in the public debt history; the Italian national debt conversion of 1906; fear of deficit financing; and government domestic debt and the risk of default.

In addition, Dornbusch and Edwards (1991) have recently edited a volume of proceedings of a conference held in 1989 that deals with problems of domestic public debt management and their implications for financial stability under conditions of high public debt and deficits. The contributions by leading scholars in the field present theoretical, empirical, and historical studies of this important policy issue.

Dornbusch and Edwards (1991) emphasise the risk of confidence crises associated with the existence of large public debts. It is argued that as the public debt becomes bigger, creditors request shorter maturities (or index debt) because of the increased default risk. The ensuing shortening of maturities, however, brings a risk of a confidence crisis. While higher interest rates might compensate creditors for such risks and avoid a crisis, they might also increase the likelihood of a crisis because they lead to a higher rate of growth of the debt. Formal models of a confidence crisis are presented by Giavazzi and Pagano (1990) and Alesina, Prati and Tabellini (1990). It is shown how the optimal management of the debt maturity might help to avert one. In essence, the models suggest that the risk of a crisis is reduced if the maturities are not concentrated on a few dates so that a similar amount of debt matures in each period; this implies that long-term debt should be preferred to short-term debt.

The key issue of institutional co-ordination of public debt and monetary management is covered in depth in Sundararajan, Dattels and Blommestein (1997). The book contains an essay on co-ordination in transitional economies and eight case studies, all of them of advanced economies.

A number of models of domestic public debt management are proposed in the literature. Bertocchi (1993) proposes a model of public debt management where government bonds are placed through 'subscription issues' and the demand for bonds is not directly observed by the authority. The debt manager selects an optimal pricing policy which maximises profits subject to an intemporal budget constraint. The ratios produced by the discrepancies between estimated and actual demand reveal valuable information about unobservable market conditions. By applying results from the theory of 'active learning' it can be shown how the price adjustment process reaches a steady state. However, it may not converge to the full information price associated with complete learning. In the long run, ratios are zero on average.

In another innovative model, Kesselman (1992) has shown that by implementing new methods of debt management, the government of Canada could significantly reduce its largest outlay, domestic public debt service costs. The model is used to assess the advantages, operation, and economics of one such innovation, namely of issuing USdollar denominated treasury bills (USDTBs) for domestic debt. It is found that average annual savings from USDTBs could range from $250 million to more than $1 billion, depending upon how they were applied and economic circumstances. Any exchange rate losses would be more than offset by the interest savings. Exchange risks would be justified by the reduced risks associated with the total public deficit – the sum of debt service charges plus the fiscal operating deficit. Reducing debt service costs through USDTBs is shown to be more attractive than most other means of curbing the budget deficit.

Another possible model is the cost minimisation model. Boothe and Reid (1992) examine the consequences of using cost minimisation as the goal of public debt management in a small open economy. Authorities are assumed to minimise interest costs subject to constraints on their ability to refinance at different maturities, and the information conditioning expectations of future interest rates. A numerical simulation model and a highly disaggregated Canadian data set for the period 1967–87 are used in the analysis. It is found that, conditional on the small open economy assumption, savings do result from following a cost-minimising strategy. Savings decline as authorities are increasingly constrained in their refinancing choices. However, even the gains in moderately-constrained cases suggest that cost minimisation is worthy of serious consideration by authorities.

Another useful domestic public debt management model involves exploiting the relationship between debt maturities and financing strategies. Goudswaard (1990) studies financing strategies that underlie the maturity structure of the public debt. Three important objectives for domestic public debt management are distinguished: interest cost reduction, economic stabilisation, and economic neutrality. The strategies that can be associated with these objectives are incorporated in a simple debt management model, which has been tested empirically for the case of the Netherlands. Variations in debt maturities between 1960 and 1985 appear to be related to changes in capital market conditions, investment preferences, and expected real interest rates.

Further, in Calvo and Guidotti (1990), optimal management of the public debt is explored in a context where economic policy is continuously revised because, when the public debt is non-indexed, policy-makers are tempted to use inflation (seignorage and inflation tax) in order to reduce the real value of the public debt. The model's implications are explored following two approaches. First, the effects of various exogenous disturbances are examined by means of numerical simulations. Secondly, the analysis explores if the model's implications concerning the maturity structure of government debt are consistent with actual experience.

The literature also presents politically motivated models for manipulating domestic public debt. It is argued that governments facing elections may strategically manipulate policy instruments in order to increase their re-election chances. For example, Milesi and Gian (1995) study the incentives for strategic manipulation in the context of a debt management model, in which two parties with different inflation aversion compete in elections. It is shown that the inflation-averse party may issue nominal debt in order to make its opponent 'look bad' to voters, thus getting closer to the median voter. Nominal debt artificially enlarges the ex-post inflation tax base, causing higher inflation. Conversely, an inflation-prone government may issue indexed debt in order to reduce inflation incentives.

Finally, but most importantly, special attention should be paid to the models used in the corporate finance literature for the valuation and pricing of bonds in the short-run and long-run (see, for example, Brealey and Myers, (1991) ch. 4). These models predict that as time tends to infinity (in the long run), the value of the bond (debt) tends to zero, as long as the debt has been continuously serviced. Researchers studying international debt have applied similar principles to determine the pricing and amortisation of debt, and in particular to explore the conditions for national solvency – see, in particular, Ghatak and Levine (1994). We believe that these same models for bond valuation could be applied to study government instruments issued for domestic public debt, in order to get a handle on the parameters for interest rate (return) determination, servicing, structuring, and retiring of existing debt as well as contracting new debt.

Background reading and references

Aghion, P. and P. Bolton (1990) Government domestic debt and the risk of default: a political-economic model of the strategic role of debt. In: Dornbusch, R. and M. Draghi (1990), pp. 315–45.

Alesina, A., A. Prati and G. Tabellini (1990) Public confidence and debt management: a model and a case study of Italy. In: Dornbusch, R. and M. Draghi (1990), pp. 94–118.

Alexander, W. E. et al (1995) *The Adoption of Indirect Instruments of Monetary Policy*, IMF Occasional Paper 126, Washington DC.

Bertocchi, G. (1993) A theory of public debt management with unobservable demand, *Economic Journal*, 103(419), pp. 960–74.

Boothe, P. and B. Reid (1992) Debt management objectives for a small open economy, *Journal of Money, Credit, and Banking*, 24(1), pp. 43–60.

Brealey, R. A. and S. C. Myers (1991) *Principles of Corporate Finance*, New York: McGraw-Hill (Fourth Edition).

Broker, Gunther (1993) *Government Securities and Debt Management in the 1990s*, Organisation for Economic Co-operation and Development, Paris.

Buiter, W. (1992) *Principles of Budgetary and Financial Policy*, New York and London: Harvester Wheatsheaf.

Calvo, G. A. and P. E. Guidotti (1990) Indexation and maturity of government bonds: an exploratory model. In: Dornbusch, R. and M. Draghi (1990), pp. 52–82.

Calvo, G. A. & M. S. Kumar (1993) *Financial Sector Reforms and Exchange Arrangements in Eastern Europe*, IMF Occasional Paper, Washington DC.

Carlo Cottarelli (1993) *Limiting Central Bank Credit to the Government – Theory and Practice*, IMF Occasional Paper 110, Washington DC.

Dornbusch, R. and M. Draghi (1990) (eds) *Public Debt Management: Theory and History*, Cambridge; New York and Melbourne: Cambridge University Press.

Dornbusch, R. and S. Edwards (1991) (eds) *The Macroeconomics of Populism in Latin America.* A National Bureau of Economic Research Conference Report, Chicago and London: University of Chicago Press.

Easterley W. and K. Schmidt-Hebbel (1993) Fiscal deficits and macroeconomic performance in developing countries *World Bank Research Observer*, Vol. 8, No. 2.

Economic Development Institute of The World Bank (1993) *Financial Sector Reforms in Asian and Latin American Countries.*

Euromoney (1996) The jugglers of sovereign debt, June 1996 pp. 91–96.

Fisher Stanley and William Easterly (1990) The economics of the government budget constraint, *World Bank Research Observer*, Vol. 5, No. 2, pp. 127–42.

Gale, D. (1990) The efficient design of public debt. In: Dornbusch, R. and M. Draghi (1990), pp. 14–47.

Ghatak, S. and P. Levine (1994) The adjustment towards national solvency in developing countries: an application to India, *Journal of International Development*, 6 (4), pp. 399–414.

Giavazzi, F. and M. Pagano (1990) Confidence crises and public debt management. In: Dornbusch, R. and M. Draghi (1990), pp. 125–43.

Goudswaard, K. P. (1990) Determinants of public debt maturity, *De-Economist*, 138(1), pp. 33–46.

Guidotti P. and M. S. Kumar, (1991) *Domestic Public Debt of Externally Indebted Countries*, IMF, Washington DC.

International Monetary Fund (1996) *World Economic Outlook*, May 1996.

International Monetary Fund (1987) *Theoretical Aspects of the Design of Fund Supported Adjustment Programs*, IMF Occasional Paper 55, Washington DC.

International Monetary Fund (1991) *Domestic Public Debt of Externally Indebted Countries*, IMF Occasional Paper 80, Washington DC.

Kesselman, J. R. (1992) Innovation in public debt management to reduce the federal deficit, *Canadian Public Policy*, 18(3), pp. 327–52.

Kilsey, June (1995) *The New Zealand Experiment*, Auckland University Press, Auckland.

Leite, S. P. (1992) *Co-ordinating Public Debt and Monetary Management During Financial Reforms*, IMF Working Paper, 92/84, Washington DC.

Leite, S.P.L. and V. Sundararajan (1990) Issues in interest rate management and liberalisation, IMF Staff Papers, Vol. 37, No. 4.

Makinen, G. E., and G. T. Woodward (1990) Funding crises in the aftermath of World War I. In: R. Dornbusch and M. Draghi (eds), pp. 153–83.

Mathieson, Donald J. and L. Rojas-Sua'rez (1993) *Liberalisation of the Capital Account – Experiences and Issues*, IMF Occasional Paper 103, Washington DC.

Milesi, F. and M. Gian (1995) Do good or do well? Public debt management in a two-party economy, *Economics-and-Politics*, 7(1), pp. 59–78.

Miller, M. H., R. Skidelsky and P. Weller (1990) Fear of deficit financing: is it rational? In: R. Dornbusch and M. Draghi, pp. 293–310.

Missale, A. E. (1994) National Government Debt Management, unpublished PhD Dissertation, Massachusetts Institute of Technology.

Roe A. (1989) *Internal Debt Management in Africa*, Development Economics Research Centre, University of Warwick, Discussion Paper 98, April.

Scorcu, A. E. (1994) Interest rate variability and public debt management, *Politica Economica*, 10(2), pp. 211–27.

Sundararajan, V., P. Dattels and Hans J. Blommestein (1997). *Co-ordinating Public Debt and Monetary Management*, IMF, Washington, D.C.

Sundararajan V., Peter Dattels, Ian S. McCarthy, Marta Castello-Branco and Hans J. Blommestein (1994) *The Co-ordination of Domestic Public Debt and Monetary Management in Economies in Transition Issues and Lessons from Experience*, IMF Working Paper.

Tanzi, Vito and Domenico Fanizza *Budget Deficit and Public Debt in Industrial Countries*, IMF Working Paper, 95/49.

Tanzi, Vito and Mario I. Blejer *Public Debt and Fiscal Policy in Developing Countries: Aspects of Public Debt Theory and Practice*.

The Economist (1996) Caught in the debt trap, 1 April 1996, London.

Truco, M. and M. Vaugeois, (1996) Domestic Government Debt of ESAIDARM Countries Paper presented at the workshop on domestic debt held in Mbabane, Swaziland. (Not yet published).

Valantin, R. (1990) *Computer Based Systems to Meet Debt Management Information Needs*, World Bank Discussion Papers, No. 155, Washington, D.C.: World Bank.

Warner, A. M. (1992) Did the debt crisis cause the investment crisis? *Quarterly Journal of Economics*, 107(4), pp. 1161–86.

World Bank/UNDP (1989) *Africa's Adjustment and Growth in the 1980s*, IBRD, Washington.

World Bank (1990) *Debt Management Systems*, World Bank Discussion Papers 108, Debt and International Finance Division. Washington DC.

World Bank (1990) *Turkey – A Strategy for Managing Debt, Borrowings, and Transfer Under Macroeconomic Adjustment*, A World Bank Country Study, Washington DC.

World Bank (1996) *World Development Report 1996*, Oxford University Press, New York.

Appendix IV: Papers Presented at the Three Regional Workshops on Effective Domestic Debt Management Held in St. Kitts & Nevis, Sri Lanka and Kenya

Background papers

Commonwealth Secretariat: Fiscal Policy and Domestic Debt Management, Commonwealth Finance Ministers Meeting, Bermuda, 24–26 September 1996.

Economic and Legal Advisory Services Division, Commonwealth Secretariat (1996): Domestic Public Debt Management – An Overview

Economic and Legal Advisory Services Division, Commonwealth Secretariat (1996): Fiscal Developments and the Evolution of Domestic Public Debt

Economic and Legal Advisory Services Division, Commonwealth Secretariat (1996): Techniques of Domestic Debt Management

Economic and Legal Advisory Services Division, Commonwealth Secretariat (1996): Measurement of Domestic Debt and Sustainability

Economic and Legal Advisory Services Division, Commonwealth Secretariat (1996): An Analytical Framework for Assessment of Domestic Public Debt

Economic and Legal Advisory Services Division, Commonwealth Secretariat (1996): Implications of Domestic Public Debt for Monetary and Financial Market Development

Gray, Simon (1996): *The Management of Government Debt*, Centre for Central Banking Studies, Bank of England

Gray, Simon (1997): *Government Securities: Primary Issuance*, Centre for Central Banking Studies, Bank of England

Guidotti, Pablo E. and Manmohan S. Kumar (1991): *Domestic Public Debt of Externally Indebted Countries*, IMF, Washington DC

Her Majesty's Treasury and Bank of England: *Report of the Debt Management Review*, July 1995

Her Majesty's Treasury: *Debt Management Report 1997–98*, March 1997

Kalderen, L. (1996): *Institutional Arrangements for Public Debt Management Functions*

Kalderen, L. (1996): *Organisation of Information Flows Between Debt*

Managers and Market Participants – the Swedish Experience

Kock, A. D.(1996): *The Role of the South African Reserve Bank in the Development of the Secondary Market for Government Bonds in South Africa*

McConnachie, Robin (1996): *Primary Dealers in Government Securities Markets*, Centre for Central Banking Studies, Bank of England

Sundararajan, V., Peter Dattels, Ian S. McCarthy, Marta Castello-Branco and Hans J. Blommestein; (1994): *The Co-ordination of Domestic Public Debt and Monetary Management in Economies in Transition Issues and Lessons from Experience*, IMF Working Paper

Ter-Minassian Teresa (1996): *Borrowing by Subnational Governments: Issues and Selected International Experience*, IMF

Truco, Manuel (1996): Domestic Government Debt of ESAIDARM Countries, World Bank

Regional Workshop, St. Kitts & Nevis, 17–21 June 1996

Papers presented by resource persons

Jayamaha, Ranee (1996): The Role of the Central Bank in the Development of Debt Securities Markets, Commonwealth Secretariat

Venner, John (1996): Fiscal Performance and Domestic Public Debt in the ECCB Area

Country papers presented by participants

Arana, Francis: Recent Trends in Government of Belize's Domestic Debt

Brown, Jonathan: Domestic Debt Management Operations in Jamaica

Basdeo, Dax: Domestic Debt Management Operations in the Cayman Islands

Mauricette, Brenda: Domestic Debt Management Operations in St Lucia

Bonadie, Nicole: Domestic Debt Management Operations in St Vincent & the Grenadines

Bruno, E. Nicholas: Domestic Debt Management Operations in Dominica

Cornwall, Dennis: Domestic Debt Management Operations in Grenada

Derrick, Sandra: Innovative Domestic Debt Management, ECCB

Eastern Caribbean Central Bank: The Impact of Fiscal Expansion on Money, Inflation and the Balance of Payments

Lettsome, Lucia: Debt Management, The British Virgin Islands Experience

Seymour, Josephine: Domestic Public Debt Management Operations in The Bahamas

Thomas-Walters, Lenoa E. and Howard Richardson: Domestic Debt Management in St Kitts/Nevis

Weekes, Julia A.: Domestic Debt Management Operations in Barbados

Williams, Debra: Domestic Debt Management in Antigua and Barbuda

Regional Workshop, Sri Lanka, 9–13 December 1996

Papers presented by resource persons

Jayamaha, Ranee (1996): The Role of the Central Bank in the Development of Debt Securities Markets

Kumar, Raj (1996): Objectives of Debt Management in Context of Fiscal and Monetary Policy, Commonwealth Secretariat

Country papers presented by participants

Ahmed, Faruquddin: Country Paper of Bangladesh

Arshad, Harliza bin and Norazman bin Ismail: Malaysia – Developing and Managing the Economy to Success

Aslam, K. Sumaira: Country Paper of Pakistan

Busai, Michael: Country Paper of Vanuatu

Enazi, Atalina: Country Paper of Western Samoa

Hamou, Aloysius: Country Paper of Papua New Guinea

Lal, M.M.: Public Debt in India

Manchanda, R.K.: India Domestic Public Debt Management

Naseer, Ahmed and A. Zaheera: Country Paper of Republic of Maldives

Saha, K: Effective Domestic Debt Management in Bangladesh

Salini, P. Christian: Country Paper of Solomon Islands

Weerasinghe, R.: Country Paper of Sri Lanka

Regional Workshop, Kenya, 9–13 March 1998

Papers presented by resource persons

Jayamaha, Ranee (1998): The Role of the Central Bank in the Development of Debt Securities Markets, Commonwealth Secretariat

Kitili, Andrew (1998): Fiscal Development and Evolution of Domestic Debt in Commonwealth Africa, Commonwealth Secretariat

Kumar, Raj (1998): Objectives and Key Issues of Domestic Public Debt Management, Commonwealth Secretariat

Kumar, Raj (1998): Indicators and Measurements of Domestic Debt Sustainability, Commonwealth Secretariat

Place, Joanna (1998): Techniques and Intervention Instruments for Domestic Debt Management, Bank of England

Place, Joanna (1998): Institutional Arrangements for Domestic Debt Management, Bank of England

Place, Joanna (1998): Role of Central Banks in Domestic Public Debt Management, Bank of England

Country papers presented by participants

Ansah, Kwame: Country Paper of Ghana

Chojoo, Raschida: Mauritius Effective Domestic Debt Management

Domingue, Joel: Country Paper of Seychelles

Iboklene, Bruno: Country Paper of Cameroon

Kajiyanike, Meg Debra: Country Paper of Malawi Domestic Debt Management

Marenga, Sam Riruako : Country Paper of Namibia

Mlangeni, Thabisile: Domestic Debt Management in Swaziland

Mverecha, Joseph: Country Paper of Zimbabwe Effective Domestic Debt Management

Mwilwa-Malulu, Nancy Chanda: Effective Domestic Debt Management – The Case of Zambia

Onduri, Machulu Fred: Public Domestic Debt Management – The Case of Uganda

Sosseh, Ngenarr: Country Paper of The Gambia

Tsolele, Makampong: Country Paper of Lesotho

Kimani, S. N.: Country Paper of Kenya

Komu, Esta: Country Paper of Tanzania Domestic Debt Management Operations

Appendix V: Participants in Regional Workshops on Effective Domestic Debt Management

Basseterre, St Kitts & Nevis, 17–21 June 1996

Antigua
Miss Debra Williams
Budget Analyst
Ministry of Finance

The Bahamas
Ms Josephine Seymour
Research Officer
Central Bank of Bahamas

Barbados
Mr Andrew Cox
Deputy Permanent Secretary
Ministry of Finance & Economic Affairs

Miss Julia Weekes
Investments Analyst
Central Bank of Barbados

Belize
Mr Francis Arana
Economist
Central Bank of Belize

British Virgin Islands
Mrs Lucia Lettsome
Budget Analyst
Ministry of Finance

Mr Allen Wheatley
Deputy Financial Secretary
Government of the Virgin Islands

Cayman Islands
Mr Dax Basdeo
Economist
Ministry of Finance and Development

Dominica
Mr Nicholas Bruno
Deputy Accountant General
Treasury Department
Ministry of Finance

Grenada
Mr Dennis Cornwall
Deputy Director
Ministry of Finance

Jamaica
Mr Jonathan Brown
Director
Domestic Debt Unit
Ministry of Finance & Planning

St Kitts & Nevis
Mr Thomas Alexander
Economist
Eastern Caribbean Central Bank

Miss Kimmoye Byron
Statistical Clerk
Eastern Caribbean Central Bank

Miss Sandra Derrick
Eastern Caribbean Central Bank

Mr Ian Ferguson
Adviser
Eastern Caribbean Central Bank

Mr Brian Francis
Eastern Caribbean Central Bank

Mr Michael Hendrickson
Eastern Caribbean Central Bank

Miss Merva Lake
Eastern Caribbean Central Bank

Mr Howard Richardson
Ministry of Finance

Mrs Abiola Streete
Research Officer
Eastern Caribbean Central Bank

Mrs Lenoa Thomas-Walters
Ministry of Finance

St Lucia
Ms Brenda Mauricette
Accountant III
Ministry of Finance

St Vincent & The Grenadines
Ms Nicole Bonadie
Economist
Ministry of Finance, Planning & Development

Mrs Ingrid FitzPatrick
Senior Account
Ministry of Finance & Planning

Trinidad & Tobago
Ms Emily Pascal
Financial Analyst
Ministry of Finance

Resource Persons
Mrs Laura Anthony-Browne
Economist
Eastern Caribbean Central Bank

Mr Liam Ebril
International Monetary Fund

Mr Cleviston Haynes
Adviser to the Governor
Central Bank of Barbados

Dr Ranee Jayamaha
Adviser (Economic)
Commonwealth Secretariat

Mr Dev Useree
Chief Programme Officer
Commonwealth Secretariat

Mr John Venner
Deputy Director
Eastern Caribbean Central Bank

Mr Arthur Williams
Eastern Caribbean Central Bank

Colombo, Sri Lanka: 9–13 December 1996

Bangladesh
Mr Faruquddin Ahmed
Economic Adviser
Research Statistics, Monetary Management
& Technical Unit
Bangladesh Bank (Central Bank)

Mrs Kamana Saha
Senior Assistant Secretary
Finance Division
Ministry of Finance

India
Mr M M Lal
Assistant General Manager
Internal Debt Management Cell
Reserve Bank of India

Mr Ramesh Kumar Manchanda
Joint Director (Plan Finance - II)
Ministry of Finance

Malaysia
Mrs Harliza Arshad
Money Market Section
Bank Negara Malaysia

Mr Norazman Bin Ismail
Assistant Secretary
Finance Division
Ministry of Finance

Maldives
Mr Ahmed Naseer
Debt Management Section
Ministry of Finance & Treasury

Mrs Ayesha Zahira
Operations Division
Maldives Monetary Authority

Pakistan
Ms Sumaira K Aslam
Assistant Financial Analyst
Debt Management
Finance Division

Papua New Guinea
Mr Aloysious Hamou
Loans and Revenue
Department of Finance

Solomon Islands
Mr Christian Salini
Central Bank of Solomon Islands

South Africa
Mr Johan Redelinghuys
Director
Debt Management & Administration
Department of Finance

Sri Lanka
Mr C A Abeysinghe
Accountant
Banking Department
Central Bank of Sri Lanka

Mr H Amarathunga
Accountant
Banking Department
Central Bank of Sri Lanka

Mrs A H B Attanayake
Director
Dept. of Fiscal Policy & Economic Affairs
Ministry of Finance & Planning

Mrs D V S Dayawansa
Senior Economist
Public Debt Department
Central Bank of Sri Lanka

Mr P L U Dissanayake
Deputy Director
Dept of External Resources
Ministry of Finance & Planning

Mr G R Gunawardena
Director Imprest
Department of State Accounts
Ministry of Finance & Planning

Mr A Kamalasiri
Accountant
Banking Department
Central Bank of Sri Lanka

Mr D Kumaratunga
Economist
Economic Research Department
Central Bank of Sri Lanka

Mr D P Liyanage
Accountant
Public Debt Department
Central Bank of Sri Lanka

Mr A J L Peiris
Senior Economist
Economic Research Department
Central Bank of Sri Lanka

Mrs H Tennakoon
Senior Economist
Public Debt Department
Central Bank of Sri Lanka

Mrs R B Weerasinghe
Senior Economist
Public Debt Department
Central Bank of Sri Lanka

Mr S P Weerasinghe
Accountant
Public Debt Department
Central Bank of Sri Lanka

Mr P A Wijeratne
Economist
Public Debt Department
Central Bank of Sri Lanka

Mr A R K Wijesekera
Economist
Economic Research Department
Central Bank of Sri Lanka

Vanuatu
Mr Michael Busai
Research Department
Reserve Bank of Vanuatu

Western Samoa
Mrs Atalina Emma Enari
Senior Economist
International Division
Central Bank of Samoa

Zimbabwe
Mr Samunel D Kameri
Technical Division
ESAIDARM

Resource Persons
Dr A R W M M A Bandara
Senior Economist
Central Bank of Sri Lanka

Mr K G D D Dheerasinghe
Deputy Superintendent
Public Debt Department
Central Bank of Sri Lanka

Mr T S N Fernando
Superintendent
Public Debt Dept.
Central Bank of Sri Lanka

Dr Ranee Jayamaha
Special Adviser (Economic)
Economic and Legal Advisory Services
Division
Commonwealth Secretariat

Mr J M T B Jayasundara
Additional Superintendent
Public Debt Department
Central Bank of Sri Lanka

Dr Raj Kumar
Special Adviser (Economic)
Economic and Legal Advisory Services
Division
Commonwealth Secretariat

Mr A R Latter
Director
Central Banking Services
Bank of England

Mr T Morrison
Senior IMF Representative
Sri Lanka

Mr Y A Piyatissa
Special Officer
Capital and Financial Market Development
Central Bank of Sri Lanka

Dr Lalith Samarakoon
Senior Lecturer
University of Sri Jayawardenapura

Nairobi, Kenya, 9–13 March 1998

Cameroon
Mr Bruno Iboklene
Head, IT Unit
Caisse Autonome d' Amortissement

The Gambia
Ms Ngenarr Sosseh
Economist
Loans and Debt Mang. Unit
Dept. of State for Finance
and Economic Affairs

Ghana
Mr Kwame Ansah
Manager
Treasury Dept.
Bank of Ghana

Kenya
Mr D M Amanja
Economist
Treasury

Mrs Sophia N Kathuka
Economist
Treasury

Mr S N Kimani
Central Bank of Kenya

Mr N M Kiritu
Central Bank of Kenya

Mr T M Kimutai
Central Bank of Kenuya

Mrs Truphenah C Makaya
Senior Economist
Ministry of Finance

Mr J B Maina
Central Bank of Kenya

Mr O R Owino
Economist
Treasury

Mr H M Sirima
Central Bank of Kenya

Lesotho
Ms Makampong Tsolele
Finance Officer
Debt Management Dept.
Ministry of Finance

Malawi
Miss Meg Debra Kajiyanike
Division Chief
Finan. Markets Operations Dept.
Local Debt Division
Reserve Bank of Malawi

Mauritius
Ms Raschida Chojoo
Assistant Manager
Operations Office
Bank of Mauritius

Namibia
Mr Sam Riruako Marenga
Principal Accountant
Debt Management Unit
Ministry of Finance

Seychelles
Mr Joel Domingue
Chief Accountant
Ministry of Finance & Communications
Treasury

Swaziland
Miss Thabisile Mlangeni
Budget Section
Ministry of Finance

Tanzania
Mr B Elikana
Ministry of Finance

Mrs Esta Komu
Domestic Debt Division
Bank of Tanzania

Mr Jimreeves Naftal
Ministry of Finance

Uganda
Mr Machulu Fred Onduri
Economist
Macroeconomic Policy Dept.
Ministry of Finance

Zambia
Ms Nancy Chanda Mwilwa-Malulu
Financial Markets Dept./LFM
Bank of Zambia

Zimbabwe
Mr Joseph Mverecha
Economics Research and Policy Division
Reserve Bank of Zimbabwe

Participants from regional organisations
Mr K Mlambo
Senior Research Economist
African Development Bank Group
Strategic Planning and Research Dept.

Ms Anna Msutze
Director
Debt Management Programme
Macroeconomic and Financial Management
Institute (MEFMI)

Resource Persons
Mr Peter Anamyni
National Bank of Kenya

Dr Ranee Jayamaha
Special Adviser (Economic)
Economic and Legal Advisory Services Division
Commonwealth Secretariat

Mr Andrew Kitili
Chief Programme Officer
Economic and Legal Advisory Services Division
Commonwealth Secretariat

Dr Raj Kumar
Special Adviser (Economic)
Economic and Legal Advisory Services Division
Commonwealth Secretariat

Mr Peter Lewis Jones
Managing Director
Stanbic Bank Ltd. &
Chairman, Kenya Bankers' Association

Mr Reuben Marambii
Chief Banking Officer
Central Bank of Kenya

Mr Nguguna Mwangi
Economist
World Bank Office
Nairobi, Kenya

Ms Joanna Place
Deputy Director
Central Banking Services
Bank of England

Mr Anand Rajaram
Economist
World Bank Office
Nairobi, Kenya

Prof T R Ryan
Professor of Economics
University of Nairobi